W9-ANX-925

HOW TO CARE FOR YOUR NEW PET

# CARING FOR
# MY NEW
# HAMSTER

## John Bankston

**PUBLISHERS**

2001 SW 31st Avenue
Hallandale, FL 33009
www.mitchelllane.com

Copyright © 2019 by Mitchell Lane Publishers. All rights reserved. No part of this book may be reproduced without written permission from the publisher. Printed and bound in the United States of America.

First Edition, 2019.

Author: John Bankston
Designer: Ed Morgan
Editor: Sharon F. Doorasamy

Names/credits:
Title: Caring for My New Hamster / by John Bankston
Description: Hallandale, FL : Mitchell Lane Publishers, [2019]

Series: How to Care for Your New Pet

Library bound ISBN: 9781680203288

eBook ISBN: 9781680203295

Photo credits: Design elements and photos Freepik.com/Getty Images, back cover live behind the lense/Getty Images, cover Bruno Cavignaux/Getty Images, p. 3 Jane Burton/Getty Images, p. 4-5 Paul Morris/Getty Images, p. 6-7 Ricky Kharawala on Unsplash, p. 8-9 Rene Wassenbergh/EyeEm Getty Images, p. 10-11 John Evaston/Getty Images, p. 12-13 Paul Bricknell/Getty Images, p. 14-15 retales botiero/Getty Images,  p. 16 @zimbahcat on Unsplash, p. 19 Paul Starosta/Getty Images, p. 20 Kaslap/Getty Images, p. 22 Jose A. Bernat Bacete/Getty Images, p. 24-25 Steve Teague/Getty Images, p. 26 Dan Burn-Forti/Getty Images

# CONTENTS

Words in **bold** throughout can be found in the Glossary.

# Hamster History

Nearly every pet hamster in the United States is related to the same three hamsters. Less than 100 years ago, people in the United States had pet dogs and cats. They did not have hamsters. That changed in 1930. A scientist named Israel Aharoni returned from Syria with several wild hamsters. They **bred** in his laboratory in Israel. He began giving them away. A few years later, they reached the United States.

Although intended for research, the hamster's gentle nature and cute habits made them perfect pets. Today millions are related to the ones Aharoni found.

Those Syrian hamsters are the most common type. Dwarf hamsters are also popular. They have different needs from Syrian hamsters.

Hamsters are often a first pet. They are tame and friendly. They are fun to watch. They often enjoy being picked up. They aren't perfect. They can bite when they are scared. They are awake at night and sleep during the day. Still, if you learn their **habits**, they can be a great pet.

## DID YOU KNOW?

Syrians called hamsters "Mr. Saddlebags" for the way they looked with food in their mouths.

# Hamster Facts

Hamsters are rodents. They are related to other rodents, such as mice, rats, and gerbils. In North America, the beaver is the largest rodent. Rodents have very strong teeth which never stop growing.

Syrian hamsters are also called "teddy bear" hamsters or "goldens" for the color of their fur. Besides golden hamsters, there are white ones, gray ones, and black ones. They can grow to more than half a foot long. They weigh about one pound. They have very short tails and can hold food in their cheeks. Their cheek pouch goes all the way to their shoulders. They don't see very well.

The Syrian Hamster is a **subspecies**. Other hamsters include the Dwarf, the Chinese, the Siberian, and the Russian Dwarf.

## DID YOU KNOW?

When a hamster pup is born, it is hairless. Its eyes and ears are closed. But they are born with their front teeth.

# Get Ready

When your hamster comes home with you, it might be nervous. You will want it to feel comfortable. You can do this by creating a safe and welcoming space.

The first step is finding a good place to put your hamster's home. It's better to put it a few feet above the floor. That way you won't look like a scary giant.

It should not be in the sun. It is very easy for a hamster to get overheated. You also want a place away from heating vents or drafts. You don't want your hamster to get too hot or too cold.

Hamsters can be noisy at night. If you are a light sleeper, don't keep it too close to your bed. You are looking for a stable surface at least two feet long by one foot wide. Have an adult help you measure. The top of a desk, a large bookshelf, or a bureau are all good choices. When you've selected the space, clear it off. Wipe it down with a damp cloth. Then it's time to go shopping for your hamster's new home.

# Hamster Habitat

Your hamster's new home should look like the one where its wild cousins live. In the desert, hamsters often **burrow**. They construct tunnels. They transport food in their cheeks and then store it underground. Your hamster should be able to do all of those things in its new home.

The place where a hamster lives is its **habitat**. Hamsters and hamster habitats are sold together. Do your new friend a favor. Buy its home first. Getting it ready will take time. You don't want to keep your new friend waiting in its critter carrier.

Although many people buy plastic cages, they aren't the best choice. Hamsters like to chew. It's easy for them to tear off a piece and swallow it. This can make them sick. Many come with tunnels which are very hard to keep clean. Hamsters can also get stuck in small tunnels.

People who raise hamsters usually keep them in wire cages. They let in fresh air. They are easy to clean. And if you set them up well, your hamster will be happy. The cage needs to be good sized—at least one foot high, one foot wide, and two feet long. Your hamster will be active. It needs room to play.

The space in the wire should not be more than one-half inch. Hamsters are great escape artists!

After your hamster gets used to the cage, you can build on it. Hamster owners often add levels and tunnels. Just don't make it too high. Because hamsters don't see very well, they often fall.

Metal wire doesn't feel good on hamster feet. You will want to make a floor. On the bottom of the cage, set a piece of cardboard or a mat on the bottom.

Atop the flooring, scatter shredded paper. Use paper without any ink (don't use newspapers or homework)! Your hamster will love to dig in the paper. Do not use cedar or pine chips. They can make your hamster sick.

In one corner, build a bed. You can use a small cardboard box. Tear up plain white tissues or paper towels. Stuff them into the box.

In the other corner, put their food bowl. This is a small ceramic bowl. Don't use metal or plastic bowls. Make sure it is small. If you use a big bowl, you might overfeed them.

## DID YOU KNOW?

Although Syrian hamsters have to live alone, dwarf hamsters are social. They like living with each other. An aquarium with a wire mesh top for air is good for dwarfs.

There are special bottles for your hamster's water. They are usually made of metal or glass. Avoid plastic. It should have a stopper so the water doesn't run out. Keep it high enough so it doesn't spill onto their bedding.

At least once a week, you will want to get rid of the old paper and replace it. Hamsters like to be clean. You will have to help to keep them happy.

# Hamster Comes Home

Hamsters cost less than a dog or a cat. There are plenty in pet stores. Still, pet stores may not be the best place. Sometimes their hamsters aren't handled often. Sometimes the hamsters are raised with too many other hamsters. Sometimes they get sick.

Hamster experts suggest two places to get a hamster. The first is at your local animal shelter or rescue center. Shelters aren't just for dogs and cats. They take in smaller animals too. Sometimes a pet hamster has babies. Unable to care for them, people leave baby hamsters at a shelter. **Adopting** a hamster means getting an animal that was unwanted, neglected, or abandoned. It will have been checked for illness. It will often come with a hamster home or supplies

The second place to get a hamster is from a **breeder**. Buying a hamster from a breeder can cost more money. But they will have greater variety. That means they may have different types, such as dwarf hamsters. They may have different colored hamsters as well.

One great thing about breeders is they train the hamsters. This means when you get one it will be used to being handled. They will even show you how to pick up a hamster.

Hamsters often sleep during the day. That makes afternoon or early evening a good time to see them moving around. Carefully look over your hamster. It should have bright eyes. The fur should be clean, the teeth even. You will also want to notice where it was raised. If it seems dirty or crowded, it's not a good place to get your hamster. If it tries to bite, this is also a bad sign.

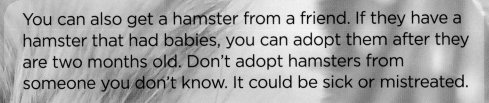

You can also get a hamster from a friend. If they have a hamster that had babies, you can adopt them after they are two months old. Don't adopt hamsters from someone you don't know. It could be sick or mistreated.

Unlike gerbils, hamsters are loners. Two hamsters in a cage will fight. If you are adopting more than one, they will need to be kept separate.

# Hamster Homecoming

At the breeder's or shelter, they will put your new hamster in a critter keeper. This is a small plastic **carrier** with a handle. Put an inch of bedding in the bottom. Add a little food in the middle.

Soon you can introduce your hamster to its new home. If you set the critter keeper carefully in the middle of their cage, you can open it and let them out.

Although you will want to play right away, give your hamster some space. It needs time to get used to its new home. You may even cover its cage with a light cloth to give it privacy. Leave the bottom part uncovered for air flow.

It will probably be awake in the afternoon when you are home from school. Never try to play with a sleeping hamster. They are grumpy when they are awakened. This is when they are most likely to bite.

Let them meet your hand first. After all, this is the part of you they will soon know best. Slowly put your hand in the cage as far from them as possible. Hamsters are curious. They investigate.

If you leave your hand in their cage for a few minutes, they will come over. You can also put food in the palm of your hand. Let them squirm over it and take a nibble. Keep your hand flat at all times.

Once they are used to your hand, you can pick them up. Be gentle. When they climb on your hand, softly place your other hand over their body. It should make a tent. Very slowly raise your hand. Bring the hamster toward your body, never away.

Be careful not to drop them. It's a good idea to have an adult help you.

*Never leave a hamster on a table or a desk. They can easily wander and fall off. Always keep them in a confined area. You might want to get a second cage for them when you are cleaning their home.*

Make sure your other pets can't come in. Hamsters and cats don't get along very well. Dogs and snakes can also be dangerous. Younger brothers or sisters should be watched if they play with your hamster.

You can use a friend or sibling to play with your hamster. Sit on the floor with your legs apart and feet touching. Let the hamster play in the space. When it tries to climb onto your leg, gently push it back. You can also blow in its face to stop them.

Once your hamster gets used to you, use your carrier to bring it to a safe space. Some hamster owners use an empty wading pool. An empty bathtub works well too. If you sit at one end, they will come over and climb over you.

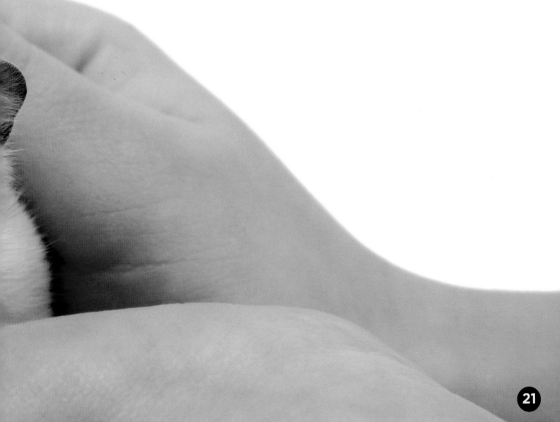

# Hungry Hamsters

Most hamsters are not picky eaters. In the wild, they eat whatever they can find. They like meat and vegetables.

The best food for the pet hamster is food made just for them. Still, food made for mice can also work. Give them about one tablespoon of pellets or seed mix once a day.

You can also give them fruits or vegetables. Have an adult slice up an apple, cauliflower, or broccoli. Wash it well. Just a small slice once a day is good.

Remember their teeth are always growing. A dog biscuit once a week can help.

Hamster treats from the pet store are good once in a while. Don't over do it. It is very easy for hamsters to gain weight.

Don't be surprised if some of the food you give your hamster winds up buried. That's what they do. It's also one reason you need to clean their cage every week.

Remember to keep their water fresh. Clean their food dish and water bottle every day. Avoid lemon scented dish soap.

# Hamsters Get Moving

Hamsters are awake for less than half of the day. They don't waste time sitting around. Hamsters love to play and exercise.

The exercise wheel is like a gym. Buy one that is solid. Hamsters can get their feet trapped in a wire wheel. If it is mesh, put tape over it. The wheel should be hamster-sized, not gerbil-sized. Make sure it's big enough for them to spin.

Let your hamster use its **instincts**. They are **foragers**. Put some food in its cage under the paper. Watch it dig.

Hamsters hide. When a hamster escapes its cage, owners often have a hard time finding it. You can keep your hamster safe and let it have fun at the same time. To do this, use an exercise ball. These plastic balls hold a hamster. When it runs inside the ball, the ball rolls around the floor. Don't leave your hamster alone, even inside the ball.

You can also use paper tubes and boxes as toys. Just make sure they are big enough for your hamster.

When your hamster gets tired, put it back in its cage. Make sure it has enough food and water. Being a hamster is hungry work.

# DID YOU KNOW?

Hamsters can sometimes make people sick. That's why it's important to wash your hands before and after playing with your hamster.

# Visiting the Vet

Just like you, hamsters need check-ups. A few days after it comes home, take it to a **veterinarian**. This special doctor only treats animals. If you have another pet, their vet can treat your hamster as well. Your hamster breeder or the shelter where you adopted your hamster will also know the name of a good one.

The vet will check your hamster's mouth. He or she will be looking for teeth that have grown too long. They'll also make sure its cheek pouches are clear. They'll check its ears, eyes, and feet. They'll gently press its belly to make sure it doesn't have any lumps. The vet will check its temperature.

The vet will also answer your questions about hamster care. He or she may tell you some good ideas for food or toys.

You can help keep your hamster healthy by playing with it often. Watch your new friend. If it seems extra sleepy or doesn't eat, that may be a sign it's sick. Some ill hamsters walk hunched over. Hair loss is another sign. If you notice any of these, make sure to tell an adult in your house. You may need to take your hamster back to the vet.

If your hamster stays healthy and happy, it still needs check-ups. You should bring it to the vet every six months. Raising a happy hamster can be very rewarding. Just try not to stay up too late watching them play.

# SHOPPING LIST

When you are ready to bring home a hamster, have an adult take you to your local pet store. This is a list of some things you will need:

- ☐ A ventilated hamster cage (not an aquarium)
- ☐ Bedding
- ☐ Nesting box
- ☐ Exercise wheel
- ☐ Ball
- ☐ Toys
- ☐ Water bottle
- ☐ Hamster chow
- ☐ Treats
- ☐ A critter keeper to bring them home

# FIND OUT MORE

## Online

There are a number of sites that will help you raise a healthy and happy hamster.

**To learn about hamster care:**

http://www.twinsqueaks.com

**The Humane Society offers advice on hamster care. The Society can also help you find shelters near you where you can adopt hamsters:**

http://m.humanesociety.org/animals/hamsters/tips/hamsters_as_pets.html

http://m.humanesociety.org/animals/hamsters/tips/hamster_housing.html?credit=web_id141921942

http://m.humanesociety.org/animals/hamsters/tips/hamster_feeding.html?credit=web_id141921942

**Petfinder connects people with adoptable animals. The online database even has a section for "small and furry" animals like hamsters.**

https://www.petfinder.com/search/small-furry-for-adoption/us

**Pet names: Here's a fun site to find a great pet name.**

https://www.bowwow.com.au

## Books

Bucsis, Gerry, and Barbara Somerville. *Training Your Pet Hamster*. Hauppauge, New York: Barron's Educational, 2012.

Ganeri, Anita. *Hamsters (A Pet's Life)*. Chicago, IL: Heinemann: 2009

Guidry, Virginia Parker, and Carolyn McKeone. *Complete Care Made Easy, Hamsters: The Ultimate Pocket Pet*. Irvine, CA: BowTie Press, 2011

Siino, Betsy Sikora. *Hamster: Your Happy Healthy Pet*. New York: Howell Book House, an imprint of Turner Publishing Co., 2006.

# GLOSSARY

**adopting**
Choosing or taking something as your own

**bred**
Produced young

**breeder**
Someone who mates animals to produce offspring

**burrow**
A hole or tunnel dug by animals for use as a hiding place or home

**carrier**
Safe container to transport an animal

**forager**
An animal that digs and searches for food

**instincts**
An inner force that causes an animal to act in a certain way

**habits**
Regular behavior

**habitat**
Natural home of an animal

**subspecies**
A particular type within a species

**veterinarian**
An animal doctor

# BIBLIOGRAPHY

Blooms, Brie. "Do Hamsters Make Good Pets for Kids?" Brie Blooms (blog), August 24, 2015. https://briebrieblooms.com/do-hamsters-make-good-pets-for-kids/.

Dunn, Rob. "The Untold Story of the Hamster, a.k.a Mr. Saddlebags." Smithsonian.com, March 24, 2011. https://www.smithsonianmag.com/science-nature/the-untold-story-of-the-hamster-aka-mr-saddlebags-1223774/#HCZDuEj0BMJSefgu.99.

"Hamsters." Healthy-pet.com. https://www.healthy-pet.com/carefresh/pet-care/hamsters.

"Hamster Care Guide." *VetBabble*. https://www.vetbabble.com/small-pets/hamster-care/.

"Hamster Feeding." The Humane Society. http://m.humanesociety.org/animals/hamsters/tips/hamster_feeding.html.

Harris, Jean. "Hamster Care Basics: Tips for New Owners." *Pethelpful*, January 24, 2018. https://pethelpful.com/rodents/hamster-care-basics.

Hertz, Lisa. "Where To Get A Hamster?" *Squeaks and Nibbles*, January 22, 2018. https://squeaksandnibbles.com/where-to-get-a-hamster/.

Imber, Davis. "Hamster Playground." California Hamster Association. http://www.chahamsters.org/qandaplayground.html.

———"Taming Hamsters." California Hamster Association. http://www.chahamsters.org/taminghamsters.html.

Magnus, Emma. "Handling Hamsters." Association of Pet Behavior Counselors (UK). https://www.apbc.org.uk/articles/handlinghamsters.

McLeod, Dr. Lianne. "Determine Whether or Not a Hamster Is the Right Pet For You." *The Spruce Pets*, March 3, 2018. https://www.thesprucepets.com/is-a-hamster-the-right-pet-for-you-1238971.

Quesenberry, Dr. Katherine E. "Providing a Home for a Hamster." *MSD Vet Manual*. https://www.msdvetmanual.com/all-other-pets/hamsters/providing-a-home-for-a-hamster.

# INDEX

# ABOUT THE AUTHOR

**John Bankston**

The author of more than 100 books for young readers, John Bankston lives in Miami Beach, Florida, with his ChiJack rescue dog named Astronaut.